[CODING YOUR PASSION™]

USING COMPUTER SCIENCE IN
HIGH-TECH
HEALTH AND WELLNESS
» CAREERS «

AARON BENEDICT
AND DAVID GALLAHER

Rosen
YA™
New York

Published in 2018 by The Rosen Publishing Group, Inc.
29 East 21st Street, New York, NY 10010

Library of Congress Cataloging-in-Publication Data

Names: Benedict, Aaron, author. | Gallaher, David, author.
Title: Using computer science in high-tech health and wellness careers / Aaron Benedict and David Gallaher.
Description: First edition. | New York : Rosen Publishing, 2018. | Series: Coding your passion | Includes bibliographical references and index.
Identifiers: LCCN 2016059443 | ISBN 9781508175155 (library bound)
Subjects: LCSH: Medicine—Vocational guidance—Juvenile literature. | Medicine—Data processing—Juvenile literature. | Computer programming—Vocational guidance—Juvenile literature.
Classification: LCC R858 .B4586 2018 | DDC 610.285—dc23
LC record available at https://lccn.loc.gov/2016059443

Manufactured in China

CONTENTS

INTRODUCTION

Information technology (IT) in the health and wellness industry is a big deal. Along with the exciting possibilities (for patients and providers) that result from their meeting, new hi-tech career paths are developing. This book exists to identify some of those options for you—to give you the chance to see, in part, what all the fuss is about.

We live in a world that is changing quickly. Those changes extend not just to our goals, but also to the skills necessary to reach them. Teachers as well as students are expected to keep up and continue learning new things. In education, there has been an increased emphasis on studies in science, technology, engineering, and mathematics (also known as STEM). In the last few years, "art" has been added, making it STEAM.

Why does STEAM deserve all this attention? Well, it's that important because STEAM applies to pretty much every part of our lives. In nearly every one of our activities in a day—from talking on a phone, to using toothpaste, to walking down a street, to keeping a schedule—STEAM is an integral part of our lives.

Basically, STEAM is what allows our lives to function with any kind of order. At the same time, it also leaves room for us to refine our ideas and to innovate so that we can improve our lives. That is a big part of

Students study science as part of the STEAM curriculum. Science courses can help give you a better understanding of the world and how things work.

why studying STEAM subjects in depth is such a smart move. Choosing this path can enable you to be con-nected, and stay connected, with something that really matters to you.

The following sections explore several different avenues for bringing your IT skills to the health and wellness industry, including specialized IT consulting, programming for computers and networking, real-time operating systems, and creating hardware for your network. (Coding examples are provided as well.)

More than anything, though, you will see how possible it is to have a viable and valuable IT career in health and wellness.

CHAPTER ONE

SPECIALIZED IT CONSULTING

No matter what the industry, IT consultants are tremendously important. They are the ones who get the internet working at the offices; verify that the network is configured and secured properly; and ensure that the computers are arranged, connected, and interconnected in all the necessary ways. Indeed, IT people do it all—they even know some programming to write scripts (small programs) and make users' lives easier. These are some tasks expected of all IT consultants on an as-needed, but constant, basis. Working in the health and wellness industry, however, requires a few additional considerations in your daily tasks.

One priority for an IT consultant is to ensure the continued health and stability of *cyberinfrastructure*; the purpose of doing so has everything to do with ensuring that both the patient and the provider are kept "in the loop"—maintaining communication between devices

The IT department is an important part of any medical facility. Computers, tablets, and phones have become life-saving devices for some patients.

and within networks is essential to providing informed and appropriate care. This extends to protecting PHI (protected health information) and maintaining patient authorizations for releases of information as required by HIPAA, which we will be discussing soon.

EMR AND EHR

Electronic medical records (EMR) and electronic health records (EHR) have become very important as technology has developed to permit them. The amount of effort that

WHAT IS CYBERINFRASTRUCTURE?

Cyberinfrastructure is the term given to every working component of a network, from servers to routers to gateways, and so on. It's basically the skeleton of the system.

At the same time, however, technology has allowed the emergence of a greater cyberinfrastructure—one that connects different electronic resources, systems, and networks into a much larger community. The goal of this larger cyberinfrastructure, it is suggested, is to have access to all existing information technology resources without the problems of distance and capability that have taken so much time in the past. Access to technology in this cyberinfrastructure will ultimately resemble access to water or roadways with those respective infrastructures.

they save can be truly extraordinary. While often used as synonyms, EMR and EHR are two different things. An EMR is something your doctor uses, within a single office/practice, to record data from your visits. With it, they are easily able easily to see how much you've grown between appointments, or the number of times that you've come in with a cold. Your EMR is useful also for determining when you should come in for a checkup.

An EHR, on the other hand, moves with the patient

from doctor to doctor, even sharing the information with labs. A good example of EHR is when your regular doctor sends you to a specialist to check something out. That specialist would then be able to see your data and the notes from your doctor and even what tests have already been conducted so the specialists don't run the same tests again. Also, the EHR allows you to log in and see the results of any tests that have been done, which can be a great time-saver for you or your parents. Using an EHR system, your doctor can send

Technology has made it easier to make appointments and communicate one-on-one with a medical professional.

a prescription to your local pharmacy so that they can have it ready for you when you arrive. This is important—the pharmacist doesn't have to try and decipher a doctor's handwriting, reducing the chance of medication and treatment errors.

Because of these benefits, EHR systems are being adopted by all hospitals, and most medical offices are starting to use them as well. They are the future,

FINDING COMMON GROUND

One fascinating and challenge to establishing online EHRs for health and wellness providers is ensuring common language, so that a patient's history can be understood by new or different providers as needed. This falls within the domain of *E/M* (evaluation and management) coding, within the International Code of Diagnostics (ICD). Although this book is primarily about IT coding within the health and wellness industry, there could very well exist another entire book about medical and diagnostic coding, as they provide detailed patient information on EHRs—to providers, medical facilities, insurance companies— in a way that minimizes the risk of breaching patient confidentiality. There is an equally promising abundance of careers in this field as well—the U.S. Bureau of Labor Statistics reports a 22 percent in a number of jobs for certified medical coders through 2022!

and the more you know about how they work, the better off you'll be. Regardless of if it is an EMR or an EHR, these services have begun moving the private data away from a computer on the network (a server of some kind), to storing the data on the internet— typically in a cloud-based system. With technology developing so rapidly, and with the number of hacks happening to e-commerce sites, what methods will best preserve privacy?

CHAPTER TWO

PATIENT RIGHTS & HIPAA

HIPAA (**H**ealth **I**nsurance **P**ortability and **A**ccountability **A**ct) is a bill signed into law in 1996 by then President Bill Clinton. The purpose of the law is for the patient (that's you) to have control over who can see their health care information. It also limits who can look at and receive your personal information. This means that, if you are visiting a new doctor, that doctor's office needs written permission from you to see your health history. In addition to giving you control about which medical offices can see your information, medical offices also have restrictions for their computers. This way, the wrong people don't have a chance to see your information. These are the kinds of restrictions that IT professionals need to know when they are working at medical offices or hospitals.

Doctor-patient confidentiality is an important part of medical care. Patients need to know that doctors and all of the technology that doctors use won't be compromised.

EMAIL AND HIPAA

Almost everyone uses email nowadays for communication in a business setting, from casual to formal. When HIPAA is involved, however, there are specific requirements and regulations to obey if you are going to use email for communication about patients. First and foremost, the emails need to be encrypted. (Let's use the analogy of a peanut butter and jelly sandwich to describe this.) If you want to tell a friend about the recipe for the best peanut butter and jelly sandwich

THE IMPORTANCE OF PRIVACY

While the privacy of medical information is likely not something given much thought these days, the danger of it being violated is a big reason why HIPAA exists. It still is the case—especially with matters of employment—that serious repercussions can occur from release of health data that is either unauthorized or fraudulent. Before the Affordable Care Act ("Obamacare") was enacted in 2010, it was extremely difficult to obtain health insurance with a preexisting condition, regardless of the details.

you've ever made, but you wish to keep it a secret between the two of you, you'd use a secret code that only the two of you know to ensure that no one else finds out. That is what encryption is, a secret code between the sender and receiver of the message.

Usually, email is not encrypted; if someone intercepts your email, they can read it. That's not a good condition for sending private patient information. For that reason, HIPAA requires encryption for any email discussing patient information.

Another requirement of HIPAA is that all email be archived and stored in a way that no one is able to access, edit, or delete any. One reason for this is that, in the event of a HIPPA violation claim, the emails

Hospital employees who have access to a patient's personal information are given training in proper email handling protocol.

must be accessible to, and viewable by, everyone. You may think that the archiving tools built into a service like Gmail are compliant with these archiving rules, but you need to do the research and not assume anything. (We all know what happens when you assume—occasionally, you're mistaken.)

Finally, there needs to be a log of everything that happens on the server, detailing which user did what and when. This is called an audit trail. Common knowledge tells us that if you don't follow a trail in the forest, you tend to become lost and not know where you are going. An audit trail is similar because it helps people find out what has happened to an email. Let's say that an email is no longer on the server. If it was deleted, which user was responsible for its deletion? At what time did that user log in to the server? Was that person even at work on that day? An audit trail can help you discover answers to those questions.

Finally, for HIPAA and email, there can be no sharing of email accounts. Everyone must have their own email account and password. The best secret is one that is known by one person. Making sure that everyone has their own email accounts and passwords makes it a little harder for someone to hack into the server. It is also important the passwords used are

POLICE PROCEDURALS

If you have read a book (or watched a show) about police and detective work, you are somewhat familiar with procedures for handling the evidence that is gathered at a crime scene. The evidence is documented; if someone comes to handle the evidence, or look at it, they need to signed in and notated. (In the justice system, this is called an *evidence chain of custody*). The same requirement applies under HIPAA regarding email—every step and event needs to be logged.

not something like "password1234"—they need to be something that a hacker won't guess immediately.

DISCLAIMERS

There is one more thing about email and privacy isn't specifically addressed in HIPAA rules and regulations; nonetheless, you will see it on every email from any organization involved in the medical field. It is a disclaimer, stating that if you are not the correct person viewing the email, you are prohibited from doing anything with the email. Here are two examples:

This email transmission is intended only for the use of the individual or entity that it is addressed to, and may contain information that is privileged, confidential, and exempt from disclosure under applicable Laws (including 45 CFR, Parts 160 & 164, Standards for Privacy of Individually Identifiable Health Information; and 42 CFR, Part 2, Confidentiality for Alcohol and Drug Abuse Patient Records and all applicable state laws). Federal rules restrict any use of the information to criminally investigate or prosecute any alcohol or drug abuse patients.

If the reader of this message is not the intended recipient, or is the employee or agent responsible for delivering the message to the intended recipient, you are hereby notified that any dissemination, distribution, or copying of this communication is strictly prohibited. If you have received this email transmission in error, please notify the sending party immediately. Thank you for your consideration for confidentiality.

Email Confidentiality Notice: This email and its attachments may contain privileged and confidential information and/or protected health information (PHI) intended solely for the use of Company Name and the recipient(s) named above. If you are not the recipient, or the employee or agent responsible for delivering this message to the intended recipient, you are hereby notified that any review, dissemination, distribution, printing, or copying of this email message and/or any attachments is strictly prohibited. If you have received this transmission in error, please notify the sender immediately at and permanently delete this email and any attachments.

Although people often simply "scroll and agree" to disclaimers, it's important to understand why they exist and your responsibility once you've agreed to the terms.

These notices are necessary for legal reasons. On occasion, you may accidentally send an email to the wrong person. This kind of disclaimer assures that it is the responsibility of the person receiving the email not to pass on any information that may be confidential. For example, imagine you are sending a text message to someone in the middle of class about a very private and personal matter. Imagine that you send it to the wrong person by mistake. You don't want the person who mistakenly received the message to spread that information all over the place. If you added a disclaimer to your text messages, the person who received it by mistake would be the one legally responsible if they spread that information about you.

CHAPTER THREE

PROGRAMMING

O ne of the more important things to know in any high-tech field is how to write programs for the computer or device you are targeting. It doesn't matter if you have an idea for the next great exercise app for iOS or Android or you are coming up with the next great health care program that all hospitals will use. That fancy new smartphone may look nice, but if there are no programs written for it (or even an operating system), the smartphone will not be very useful. When you write a program, you are basically writing in a different language—a language that the brain (processor) of the device will understand. Writing code is where you'll find the action in the high-tech world.

Now that applications can reside on websites, there are specific languages used for web programming that are not used for computers or smart devices. This chapter will discuss some of the more popular languages being used for both computers and smart devices.

Programming for an iPhone or other piece of Apple technology is different from writing programs for a piece of Windows technology. Know your hardware!

TYPES, TERMS & LANGUAGES OVERVIEW

Before we go into some of the programming languages, there are important terms that every programming language will use and should be learned before starting. To illustrate some terms, we'll revive the analogy to a peanut butter and jelly sandwich. Here are some of the more important terms and their meanings.

Algorithm: Steps taken to complete a task. Think about making a peanut butter and jelly sandwich. What are the steps you take in making a peanut butter and jelly sandwich? That is an algorithm.

Bug: An error in the program's code. Think of making that peanut butter and jelly sandwich when you are instructed to spread paste onto the bread instead of peanut butter. That would be a bug.

Command: Instructions for the computer. In making a peanut butter and jelly sandwich, the required first step is to get two slices of bread. That would be considered a command in a program.

Loop: Performing the same task repeatedly.

Variable: A placeholder for information that can change. Think once again about the peanut butter and jelly sandwich. What if you wanted to use something else instead of peanut butter (like cream cheese)? The choice between peanut butter and cream cheese would be a variable.

It is also important to know and understand the type of hardware for which you are writing your software. If you are writing it for use with any kind of smart device (phone, tablet, etc.), then you may want to consider the accelerometer (a device that measures movement and speed, allowing you to see how many steps you've taken or how many miles you've biked). If you are programming for a computer, then you will have greater processing power for your program, so you can perform more processor-intensive tasks with it, like rendering X-rays or three-dimensional images of a patient.

In the meantime, here is a rundown of some different programming languages and scripts (with a bit of the history behind each).

C

The programming language C was developed in 1972 by Dennis Ritchie, who was working for Bell Labs at the time. His 1978 publication, *The C Programming Language*, spurred a revolution in computing. C should be considered the "father" of the other languages we will be addressing here because they all are based on C in some way.

So what does a basic program in C look like? To give you an example of that, we will use what is essentially the first program anyone learns when starting to code in any language—the "Hello World" program. (We will be using the "Hello World" example for all of the programming languages discussed in this chapter.)

```
/* Hello World program */
#include<stdio.h>
main()
{
    printf("Hello World");
}
```

It doesn't look like something from a storybook,

Programs like Women Who Code teach women and girls the skills they need to write their own code and create their own programs.

does it? The reason that it doesn't resemble any language we would recognize is that it needs to talk to the computer, and the computer does not understand English, Spanish, Mandarin, Wolof, or any other human language. Computers speak *machine language*. In fact, the closer we get to programming languages looking like a language that we would recognize, the more steps will be required to convert it into machine language.

THE INVENTION OF C

What would the world of programming look like if it weren't for Dennis Ritchie creating C? For starters, the development landscape would be a lot more fragmented, with other languages filling the vacuum of C's absence. A programming language called Pascal may have been more popular. There would have also been a lot more focus on knowing Assembly, which is the lowest level of a programming language before it reaches machine language.

C++

One of the more well-respected programming languages is C++. It is still being used in new programs today, despite the emergence of languages that are more modern and easier to use. Additionally, C++ was the first object-oriented programming language to hit the mainstream and become popular with developers.

The history of C++ goes back to the early 1980s, when Bjarne Stroustrup started working on the first iteration of C++, called "C with classes." That was later changed to C++ in 1983. In 1985, Stroustrup's reference to the language, *The C++ Programming Language*, was published and soon became an indispensable reference for developers. In 1998, the C++ Standards Committee released the first international standard for the programming language.

The number of programs developed using C++ are numerous and varied. A few major examples include Microsoft Office, Windows 7 (and earlier iterations), and Adobe Photoshop. It would not be surprising if software currently being used in the health and wellness industry is also written in C++.

Here is an example of the "Hello World" program written in C++:

```
// my first program in C++
#include <iostream>

int main()
{
  std::cout << "Hello World!";
}
```

Notice that the structure looks very similar to the "Hello World" program written in C, which is because C++ is a direct descendant of C. There are some key differences, which are addressed in lots of other books (but not this one).

OBJECTIVE-C

Objective C is used by most, if not all, developers for Apple's Macintosh OS. It is also used to write programs for iOS (iPhone operating system), although the newer Swift is gaining popularity. Objective-C was developed by Brad Cox and Tom Love in the early 1980s, while the two were working for Stepstone. After creating their own company, Objective-C was licensed by NeXT (Steve Jobs' second company) and was central to the NeXT OS. After Apple purchased NeXT in 1996, it began using Objective-C to develop Mac OSX, and it has been a major part of developing on Apple's operating systems until today.

Here is an example of what a program would look like using Objective-C:

```
// First program example

#import <Foundation/Foundation.h>

int main (int argc, const char * argv[])
{
        NSAutoreleasePool *pool =
[[NSAutoreleasePool alloc] init];
        NSLog (@"Hello, World!");
        [pool drain];
        return 0;
}
```

This one might look a bit tricky, but it is widely used!

SWIFT

Consider Swift as the "little sibling' of Objective-C. Swift is a very new programming language, released in 2014 by Apple (it is now open source). It was designed to be a replacement for C-based languages, to make things easier for developers and more secure for users.

As you probably could tell from the sample Objective-C code in the previous section, Objective-C is difficult to learn. Therefore, Apple wanted to make something for new (and existing) developers that would be easy to learn and would more closely conform to the modern methods of application development. Here is an example

SWIFTLY NOW

There is something important to mention about Apple's development languages. In order to make developing for iOS (and Macintosh computers) more accessible for new developers, Apple is slowly de-emphasizing Objective-C in favor of Swift. If you are interested in programming for iOS as an independent developer writing the next great health tracker, working in a large development company, or both, it would make a lot of sense to learn Swift instead of Objective-C. In fact, Apple is making it very easy to learn Swift—Apple now has a downloadable app for iOS called Swift Playground. It is available in the iOS App Store, built only for an iPad.

of the "Hello World" program written
in Swift:

```
println("Hello, World!")
```

It is amazing how different it is from what you see in Objective-C or even C++. Once again, there are a lot of reasons for why this is, explained in other places (but not here).

JAVA

Java was developed in the early 1990s by James Gosling and others working at Sun Microsystems. Gosling and company were looking for a way to write their software once and have it run on any kind of device (specifically, cable boxes). Since the internet was just gaining popularity in 1995, Java was at the right place at the right time to

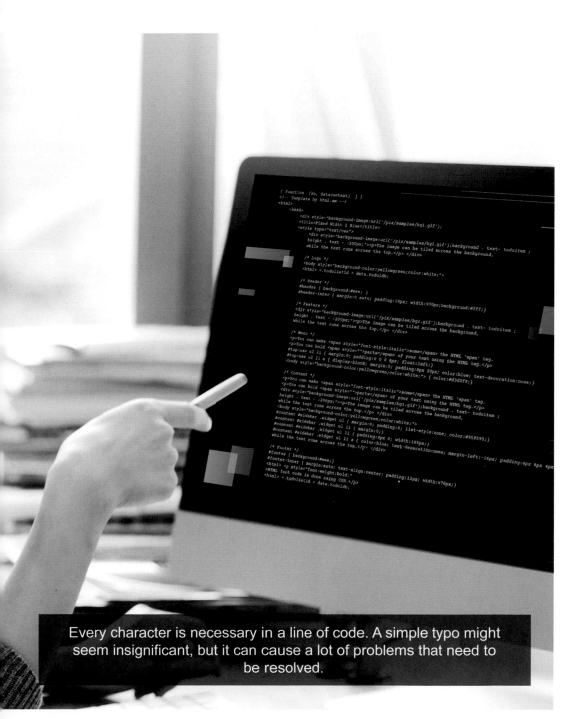

Every character is necessary in a line of code. A simple typo might seem insignificant, but it can cause a lot of problems that need to be resolved.

gain popularity with developers because of its promise to write once and run anywhere.

This kind of portability is important in the health care industry. IT consultants see many programs where Java is the backbone for many different reasons and purposes. Another reason that Java is popular is because it uses a similar syntax to C++, so developers who are familiar with C++ can learn quickly to develop software with Java.

Let's see what a "Hello, World" program looks like in Java.

```
public class HelloWorld {

    public static void main(String[] args) {
        // Prints "Hello, World" to the terminal window.
        System.out.println("Hello, World");
    }

}
```

PYTHON

Python's history starts in the 1980s. It was developed by Guido van Rossum as a tool for interfacing with an OS named Amoeba. (Van Rossum is still responsible for Python's direction, having been given the title of Benevolent Dictator for Life [BDFL] by the community.)

The interesting thing about Python is that it's not exactly a scripting language like PHP (which we'll discuss soon), but it's not exactly compiled, either. This makes it slower than some of the languages we've discussed in this chapter (see the sidebar for a quick explanation of why this is the case). However, it is one of the easier languages to learn, and the community is very helpful. Because it is easy to learn and you can do a lot with it, Python is a language that is used at many companies, and it can be used in the health and wellness industry as well. Python is the basis for the web framework Django, which you will read about in the next chapter.

Here is some example code written in Python:

```
print ("This is just a test.")
```

That is one of the most straightforward examples of code that there could ever be.

LET'S SEE YOUR SCRIPT

A special feature of both Python and Ruby is that they are also used as scripting language. Scripting is not about writing a play, TV show, or movie. It is using a language to control another application so that you won't have to do the same things repeatedly in the exact same way. If, for example, you want to resize 10 different pictures to the same size for emailing to a friend, you have two choices. You could either resize each one and attach them all to an email, or you could have a script take care of those steps for you. Writing a script like this is especially

(continued on the next page)

(continued from the previous page)

handy if you need to resize and email pictures all the time.

Scripting language does not need to be compiled. It gets interpreted into machine language on the fly, making it slower than a compiled language. All you need to do is open a text editor, write the code, save the file with the proper extension (.py for Python, .js for JavaScript, .rb for Ruby), and run to script.

RUBY

Ruby is another one of those "underdog" programming languages. It was created in 1995 by Yukihiro Matsumoto, and the intention was for Ruby to be natural but not simple. It is like Python in that it can be used both as a scripting language and to write programs. It is the heart of the web framework Ruby on Rails, which is addressed later in this book. (A fun fact about Ruby is that it was named for the birthstone of one of Matsumoto's colleagues.)

Here is an example of the "Hello World" program written in Ruby:

```
puts 'Hello world!'
```

Once again, that is a fairly simple example of code writing, but it's a lot simpler than some of the other examples we have seen in this chapter.

PROGRAMMING FOR THE WEB

I know that this is hard to believe, but there was once no internet. There was even a time in which there was the internet, but you had to use a phone line to get to it, and believe me when I tell you that the connection was very, very slow. Now the internet is everywhere, and it is fast enough for people to connect to it from anywhere. It's not a surprise that the web has taken off like it has. Because of that, people have been building programs that use the accessibility of a web site to build programs for anything from a database to record the comic books you have and you've read to tracking your daily calories and weight.

Website development is generally divided into two parts: the front end, which is how the site will look to the user; and the back end, which is where a lot of the heavy lifting and database work happen. The front-end work is usually done with something called Cascading Style Sheets (CSS) and/or Hypertext Markup Language (HTML, now up to version 5). In this section, we are going to focus on some of the back-end languages that developers are using to get their work done. If you would like to learn more about the front-end work that goes into designing what a site or web application looks like, please see the back of the book for a reference or two.

In the early days of web programming, tasks were performed using a Common Gateway Interface (CGI). The programs were written in either C or another language called PERL (either Practical Extraction and Report Language or Pathologically Eclectic Rubbish Lister, depending upon your mood). As web server technology has advanced, the need to use a CGI has changed in addition to the languages that may have to be used for the CGI. If it were not for these advancements, a web developer would still be focused on writing in PERL (and may have gone insane).

PHP

PHP is a scripting language that works in a web page's HTML code. The code is only seen by the

WEB SERVERS

"I will be your server this evening."
    Web servers are just that. They are computers that specialize in making sure your website (or web-based application) delivers the necessary files and components to the user's web browser. Think of a web server as a waiter at a restaurant and the web browser as the customer. The customer tells the waiter what they want, and it is then up to the waiter to deliver their requests properly and promptly. While a web server never receives a tip from a browser, it will never put its fingers into the browser's soup.

web server and the results are displayed on the web page as HTML. PHP was developed in 1994 and originally stood for "Personal Home Page." In 1997, it was rebuilt by Zeev Suraski and Andi Gutmans, and the meaning of PHP was changed to PHP: Hypertext Preprocessor. PHP is now being used to power anything from blogs to major websites.

Here's an example of a simple PHP script:

```
<!DOCTYPE html>
<html>
<body>

<?php
echo "My first PHP script!";
?>

</body>
</html>
```

As you can see from the first line, the start is in HTML. Then you get to the script; when that is run, the words "My first PHP script!" will be written on the web page. This is just a basic example, but it can be used in more powerful ways. For example, on a health-focused recipe site, it can be used to show you all the recipes that use kale; if it were a website that tracks calories for you, then it could show you how many calories you have eaten that day and how many you have left within your targeted range.

RUBY ON RAILS

Ruby on Rails is a programming language and environment for creating web-based applications (also called a web application framework). Services and sites such as Airbnb, SoundCloud, and Hulu all have been developed using Ruby on Rails. It is also used by the company Optum, a software company in the health care industry that focus on processing insurance claims.

It was created by David Heinemeier Hansson, who first used it to create a project management tool called Basecamp. In 2004, he split the language and environment off from the Basecamp application and dubbed it Ruby on Rails. It is designed to be able to develop the software quickly.

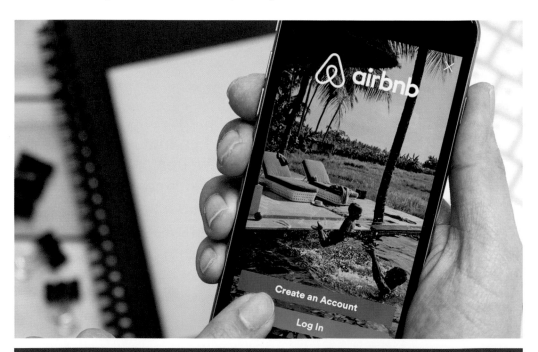

There are apps for almost everything these days! Apps give you a more contained experience, without having to access a company's website.

An example of the "Hello, World" code for Ruby on Rails would look like this:

```
class ApplicationController < ActionController::Base
  protect_from_forgery with: :exception

  def hello
    render html: "hello, world!"
  end
end
```

As you can see, it is more difficult than PHP, but that isn't all that's required to get Ruby on Rails to generate "Hello World." There are a lot more steps to get it started; if you are interested, you can check out some of the sites provided at the end of the book to learn more about the language and framework.

CAN I SEE YOUR LICENSE PLEASE?

When it comes to web development (and regular development), a good number of the languages used are under what is called an open source license. What this means for you is that it is free to download and use. However, depending on the type of license used, there may be some restrictions as well. It is always good practice before using open-source

(continued on the next page)

(continued from the previous page)

software to investigate what license is being used and what that means for you as a developer. This is opposed to a commercial license where you must buy the software to use the software. An example of this would be needing to buy Microsoft's Visual Studio to use its version of C++.

JAVASCRIPT

Even though it shares the word "Java," don't confuse JavaScript with the programming language Java, for they are nothing alike. In fact, JavaScript was originally named LiveScript, but it was changed to JavaScript in 1995 to take advantage of Java's rapid popularity. JavaScript has been called "the glue language" that makes it easier for web developers to do things. Because it is such an important part of website development, it should be learned if you are going to be doing any web-related development.

This should be familiar to you by now—an example of "Hello World":

```
<!DOCTYPE html>
<html lang="en">
  <head>
    <title>Some Page</title>
    <script type="text/javascript">
```

```
    alert("Hello World!");
   </script>
  </head>
  <body>
   <p>The content of the web page.</p>
  </body>
 </html>
```

If this code is in a browser, an alert box saying "Hello World!" will pop up in the browser.

DJANGO

Django has an interesting history. It was developed in 2003 for a newspaper, the *Lawrence Journal-World*. Two developers, Adrian Holovaty and Simon Willison, were using Python to build applications. Because newspapers are deadline-driven, their websites are as well. Holovaty and Willison developed a time-saving web development framework because it was the only way they could build maintainable applications under the extreme deadlines they were always facing. If it were not for Holovaty and Willison's development of Django, many news sites might still be using older ways of developing web applications.

Because it was originally developed for newspapers, Django is very focused on content. Because of this, sites like The Onion, Pinterest, and Instagram all use it. Although only recently making inroads, it is easy to see how Django would be useful to the health and wellness industry.

Here is the "Hello World" sample code from Django:

```
from django.http import HttpResponse

def hello(request):
    return HttpResponse("Hello world")
```

WHAT ARE WEB FRAMEWORKS ANYWAY?

You now have heard the phrase "web frameworks" at least twice in this book. You may be asking yourself: "Hey, Self! What are web frameworks anyway?" Simply speaking, a web framework makes it easier for you to develop your application. Most sites have a common set of functionalities (like handling sessions, data validation, etc.), and a framework is something that keeps you from having to rewrite them every time you create a website. This means that as a developer, you can create websites faster and more easily by using frameworks. Frameworks are the third generation of web development. The first generation was writing each web page in HTML. The second was the use of scripting languages, like PHP or JavaScript. The third generation is the use of web frameworks to create the site. What will the fourth generation of web development look like? Only time will tell.

Web programming has many uses. You may have an idea for a new health care site, or you develop software for a hospital that uses an internal website for the delivery of the software. Either way, there are several different languages that can be used in order to create and refine software. There are also two parts to web development—the front end and the back end. The front end is the look and feel of the site. The back end refers to storing the data and how the data can be found.

CHAPTER FOUR

REAL-TIME OPERATING SYSTEMS AND HARDWARE

010
101
001
010
010
010
110
010

T wo questions for you:

What is a Real-Time Operating System (RTOS)? Why would a RTOS be so important in the health and wellness industry?

Let's answer the first question first. We are all familiar with operating systems that your computer, phone, or tablet uses. The operating system makes sure the computer runs, allows you to run your applications and manage your files. Some operating systems allow this more than others. For example, iOS allows you to manage your files only within the scope of an application; even then, it provides very basic functionality, which is something that many high-end users dislike about iOS.

A real-time operating system is focused on providing the application and hardware the resources necessary to do a job without having to prioritize. The

010
010
001
010
010
010
110
010

"real-time" part of the name does not mean that the system responds quickly; it just means that there are rigid time requirements that must be met. If these time requirements are not met, your results can become inaccurate or unreliable. Delays are usually measured in tenths of a second.

An RTOS is not used in a regular personal computer. (When the term "personal computer," or "PC," is used, we are talking about a computer that runs on Windows, Mac OS, and even Linux. They all are used on personal computers. It is a bit of a pet peeve that people draw a distinction between a PC and a Mac, for the reality is that they are *all* PCs.) In the health and

Computer users tend to be either PC or Mac users exclusively. But there are benefits to each.

wellness industry, it is used in devices like sonograms, X-ray machines, insulin pumps, and others. Non-medical devices that use a RTOS are digital cameras, mobile phones that are not smartphones, and some of the smart devices in your homes (known as the "Internet of Things"). Anywhere that a device has one specific use and you need to turn it on, it is likely to be running with a RTOS.

An alternate name for a RTOS in this context is an *embedded system*. This is because the software is embedded into the hardware for a specific job to be done. Another characteristic of an embedded system is that there is little or no interface for operating the hardware. The input to the RTOS is not done via keyboard and mouse like it's done with a desktop computer. The input is done from sensors connected to the hardware.

Now that we have answered the first question, let's answer the second question. Why are real-time operating systems important for devices in the health and wellness industry? The reason is quite simple: they are widely used in the health and wellness industry. When you are dealing with a device that is doing something important, and you want to make sure that it will work and not have random crashes, you will require a RTOS. Often, it is the case that someone has their life depending on the function of the device. Imagine a friend of yours is diabetic and has an insulin pump that provides them with the correct amount of insulin when they need it. If the pump were to fail in some way, the effect on your friend would be harmful

OPERATING SYSTEMS

In addition to meeting the rigid time requirements, a real-time operating system also needs to respond reliably in an unpredictable event. Let's go back to the example of a friend with an insulin pump. The designer of the RTOS and the hardware need to have a way to be sure that if something weird or unexpected happens (like the pump becoming disconnected from your friend), the pump won't just continue to pump insulin (which wouldn't be good). For situations like this, the developer would program the pump to turn off automatically and emit a sound, notifying your friend that something has malfunctioned. Your friend could then fix the problem.

and could be deadly. This is a circumstance that the device itself is designed to avoid, and it is the reason a real-time operating system is needed. It does one thing, and it does that one thing really well.

GETTING STARTED

There are many different versions of real-time operating systems out there. Many of them are proprietary, meaning that the source code behind them is not available to be seen unless you buy the rights to the operating system. However, there are some open-source RTOS out there. It is interesting to note that there are at least 25 active open-source projects that are RTOS. There are another nine that are not currently under active development, which means that they have not been worked on in at least two years. At any rate, that's a lot of operating systems. This means that you can look at the source code and try to understand what the operating system is trying to do. To understand the source code, you will need to understand a programming language. Most of the time, the code of a RTOS will be written in C. Therefore, having some knowledge of programming languages will be helpful. Also, you should have a teacher or someone else walk you through some of the harder parts of the source code. That will be helpful as well.

The first step to take is downloading the source code from the project's website. You will also need to download an emulator to run the source code on your computer. An emulator (also known as a "virtual machine") is software for your computer that enables one computer system (called the host) to mimic another computer system (called the guest). Using an emulator allows you to have a virtual device that is powered by a RTOS on your computer. This way, you can test the RTOS source code (and any changes you may have made) to see how it reacts without spending a lot of money on hardware that might not even work if the OS is disrupted.

An alternative is to buy an inexpensive piece of hardware that runs a RTOS and test it on that. An example is a device called Raspberry Pi. A third alternative (and maybe the best one) is to learn the Arduino programming language at the website circuits.io. The cool thing about that site is that it has a built-in emulator with which you can make things light up, move, or even explode (if you tell anyone about this, be sure to mention that the explosions are only virtual). Although it is a membership site, it is free to sign up and use.

SUMMARY

A real-time operating system (also known as an embedded system) is a system that expects feedback in a timely fashion. Because a RTOS usually does one thing really well, it is important to the health and wellness industry. A RTOS is used in lots of difference devices, including sonograms, glucose monitors, cardio machines, and electrocardiogram devices. There are several ways to learn how to work with a RTOS, including emulators and a website where you can make things virtually explode (if you're into that sort of thing).

HARDWARE

Many services in the health and wellness industry rely on hardware. From the activity tracker on your wrist to

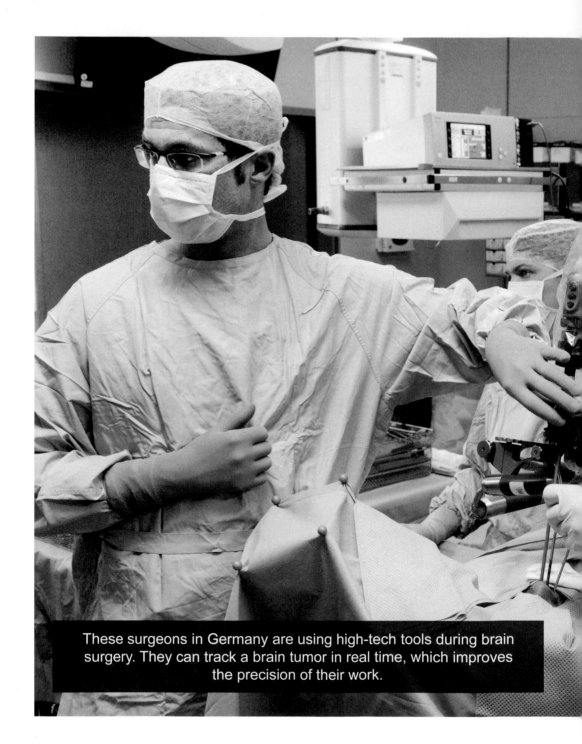

These surgeons in Germany are using high-tech tools during brain surgery. They can track a brain tumor in real time, which improves the precision of their work.

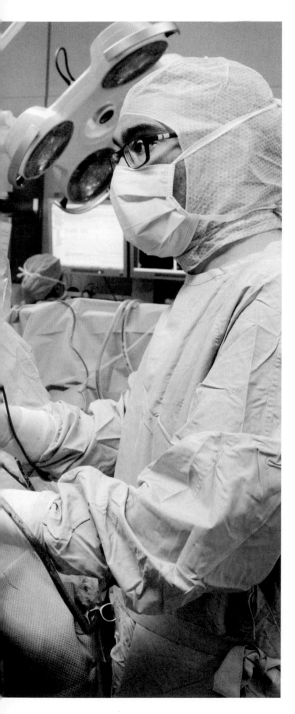

dialysis machines, and everything in between—it's all a matter of hardware. In truth, many of the concepts and ideas detailed in past chapters tie into this chapter about hardware. The reason for this is because when you create the hardware. it is going to need to know what to do. Even if you build an exoskeleton for someone who is paraplegic and connect it to their brain, the hardware will still need some interface to know what to do. To get that done, you will need to know something about operating systems that work in real time and understand how to do some programming.

What is the best way to get started learning more about electronics? The best way to start learning about electronics is to get a

HARDWARE, SOFTWARE— WHAT'S THE DIFFERENCE?

By now you will have heard of hardware and software. The difference between the two is very simple. Software is a program that is written for various operating systems (for example, Microsoft Word will work on computers that run either Microsoft Windows or Apple's Mac OS). Other software programs perform other functions on different, specified operating systems. Hardware, though, is the actual, physical device (or part of that device) that runs the operating system and other programs. Even the operating system is considered software!

breadboard. "What does bread have to do with electronics?" you might be asking. That is a very good question. In electronics, a breadboard is an experimental test circuit board—something used to build circuits. Back when electronics were much larger than they are now, people took breadboards from their kitchens and used them to mount what they needed to build a circuit. Parents everywhere balked at having nowhere left to slice bread. Even though we've since devised better circuit boards, the nickname of "breadboard" has stuck.

When beginning to learn about electronics and hardware, the breadboard (or experimental test circuit board) is the best place to start. This is because it will allow you to experiment and see how a circuit that you designed will react. Breadboards can be used for circuits of any level of complexity. Getting started with a breadboard is a simple thing to do, and they are widely available at little expense (a quick search on Amazon showed one for $5.99 [including shipping]). These packages come with tutorials that walk you through using the breadboard, even giving you projects as you go.

In addition to the breadboard and the tutorial, the package also comes with some of the parts needed to create circuits. Those parts include LEDs of different colors, a motor, on/off switches, capacitors, resistors, transistors, jumper wires, and a dot-matrix display. (It is important to note that different packages will contain different parts. Please check to see what you are getting in your order.) You can also use the circuits.io website that we mentioned in the last chapter to do some of these things virtually, especially the explosions.

There are some terms and concepts you will need to know in order to learn about hardware creation. These are the fundamentals of going forward with making hardware.

Microcontrollers The brains of the hardware, allowing the hardware to "think."

Sensors The eyes and ears of the hardware, also able to record data.

Storage Where you store the operating system and recorded data from sensors.

Voltage The direction in which electrons would flow if two wires were connected.

Current The amount of energy flowing through the path in a circuit. Consider thinking about it in relation to how fast water goes through a pipe to get to your shower. Lots of water pressure is a high current; low water pressure is a low current.

GETTING STARTED

Let's say you have an idea for the next great wearable health-monitoring tool. Your device is going to make anything that has come before it look like a stone by comparison. How do you go from your idea to getting the hardware made? Before it can become the Next Big Thing, there are several necessary steps to complete.

Come up with the idea. You've already done that part, so congratulations! At this stage, it is good to envision and capture what you would like the finished hardware to look like.

Design the product. Now that you have the idea and know what you want it to look like, it is time to get to work designing the product. At this point, you may be using a computer aided design (CAD) program to help you start making your dream a reality. The CAD program will allow you to create parts, place and move them around on a canvas, and connect their pins together. Your goal with this is to go from a blank canvas, to a set of building blocks, to a fully connected logical

Wearable health-monitoring tools have increased in popularity in the last several years. People can track exercise, heart rate, and even blood sugar levels.

design. This logical design should "work." It should generate power from other power, activate all parts that need power in the correct order, and connect to abstract inputs and outputs. There will be a lot of starts and stops in this stage of the process. Your original idea may not work exactly the way you want it to. Rather than be discouraged by that, just remember that this happens to every inventor. Very few human achievements in life occur without trial and error. Once you've developed something that works in theory, you have "the concept." One thing to remember here: the more time spent getting things right at this stage, the better the next stage will be for everyone.

Make sure it works. Now that you have the concept all ready, it's time to make sure what works in theory will work in the real world. This is called the prototype stage. You typically need to buy several prototypes to test different things (like whether it will turn on and off). This stage may also have several cycles, just like designing it did.

Production. Finally, your health-tracking device is ready to share with the world and hopefully start a company and make lots of money. Good Luck!

SUMMARY

Creating hardware is a multidisciplinary endeavor. In addition to needing an understanding how electronics work, you will need to understand coding and the theory behind RTOS. You need either to understand all of it or partner with people who can help you make your dream happen. Additionally, there is a process that happens, once you come up with the idea, in order to get your product to market. Don't forget that sometimes, failures do occur—but learn from failures instead of being discouraged by them. That advice applies also to software development. As Albert Einstein once said, "Failure is success in progress."

CHAPTER FIVE

SECURITY

In the health and wellness industry, the need for security is underscored by how quickly things are changing. When systems or applications are being updated or upgraded, when users and administrators have to learn new techniques and systems, or when transferring and translating patient information between storage types, moving from private storage to a cloud-based format—these are the moments in which mistakes can occur and when the network is most susceptible to attack from hackers or viruses.

Hackers understand the sensitive nature of PHI (protected health information) and PII (personally identifiable information), and know that there are serious consequences to HIPAA violations. (Indeed, financial penalties can go up to $1.5 million for HIPAA violations, to say nothing of the potential criminal charges involved.) That sensitivity is what makes the information valuable to them and makes it desirable to hacking a health-based network.

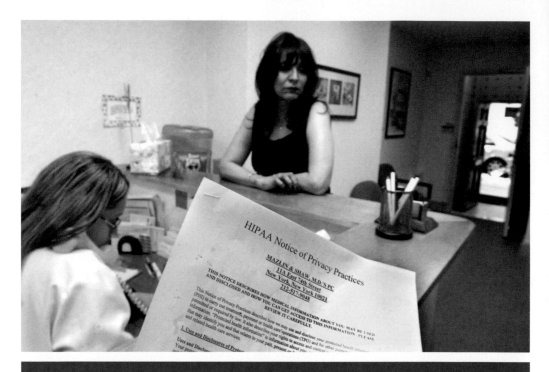

This doctor's office in New York has been remodeled to help protect patient privacy under HIPAA. Even an accidental glance at another patient's record might be considered a crime.

NETWORK SECURITY

With HIPAA and the growing necessity of data integrity in the conversion to EHR, a primary concern in the health and wellness industry is ensuring network security. This entails securing the network from not only threats originating outside the network (external), but also threats that may come from inside the network (internal).

Coming from inside of the network is something along the lines of making sure every person has their

ARE YOU UP TO DATE?

An important part of HIPAA for both email and network security is to keep the network's anti-virus software updated. This must be monitored on the mail server and across the network. One of the foremost ways in which viruses can propagate, and hacking can occur, is through email. Typically, it all starts with a friendly looking message from a personal or professional contact, requesting that you check out a new site. Or you could receive an email from a provider of some sort (a bank, PayPal, Netflix, your computer's manufacturer), telling you of a serious problem with your account that you can begin to fix by clicking on the link provided. In either scenario, the email (or the website) may look legitimate. But it is owned by hackers, who will then use the fake site to install software onto your machine. That software will permit the hackers access to all of your passwords.

In addition to the anti-virus software being up to date, it is also a good idea to train everyday users of your network's software to be on alert for these kinds of attacks. The more they know, the safer you all will be from hacking.

own account to log in to, just like is required by email. It is also good practice to have each user's password be unique to the user and not the same for everyone.

Another important thing to look at for securing the network from inside attacks is that the screen saver should go off after about three to five minutes of inactivity and users should lock the desktop, manually start the screen saver, when they walk away from the desk. Once the screen saver is activated, it should not be able to be deactivated unless a password is entered. This protects against any would-be snoopers while someone is away from the computer.

External attacks need to be prevented as well—perhaps even more so than internal ones. We have all heard of big companies and even federal government agencies, like the Internal Revenue Service and the US Office of Personnel Management, being broken into

President Barack Obama met with his national security team in February 2016 to discuss cybersecurity. Older computers might be to blame for government information leaks.

with horrible results. Using a device situated between the internet connection and the network—a firewall—will help make sure that attacks on the network fail. Something else the firewall can usually do is ensure that people can go only to a limited number of allowed, legal sites. For example, if a hacker sends an email instructing to visit a website, and the site is not an approved or "whitelisted" site, then the hacker will not be able to get passwords or access to computers.

A PERSONAL TALE

If you don't think this is something that can happen, rest assured it does. Last year I personally had to deal with an attack involving *ransomware*. This is when a hacker gets access to the data on the computer and encrypts it. The hackers then inform you that in order to decrypt the files, you must pay money, with the amount increasing every day or so. I was called in to clean up the mess and it was a lot of work; although I eventually got most of the data back for my client, it wasn't perfect and they still had a lot of work to do on their own.

THREAT AND RISK ASSESSMENTS

As an IT professional in the health and wellness industry, it is of the utmost importance to maintain network security. This we know. But how does one determine the best way to direct resources in providing that security? The answer to that is in having frequent threat and risk assessments.

Before we go into that, it's important to distinguish between a risk and a threat in the context of security. Basically, it goes like this:

The inside (you) creates the risks—whether through

In 2015, UCLA Medical Center reported that hackers might have had access to medical data. The hack affected as many as 4.5 million people.

distraction, lack of training, absent-mindedness, etc.

The outside presents the threat—be it a competi-
tor, an angry customer, an aspiring cyberthief, etc.
Being able to minimize risks is every bit as important
as guarding against threats. If the two ever happen to
coincide, look out!

Performing a threat and risk assessment almost
always involves an IT consultant because the network
needs examining through fresh, unbiased eyes. Also,
the assessment extends beyond physical security of
the network—there exists a great deal of fact-finding
about the workers, the work environment, the services provided, and much more. During this process,
many questions are addressed and answered: Are the
employees overworked? Is there any history of medication or privacy errors? How is the company viewed by
the community? Many of these factors are considered
and contribute to a relatively complete understanding
of the network's vulnerabilities. Through this process,
there emerges a very clear picture (sometimes, liter-
ally) of where to allocate security resources, as well
as where to be mindful about improving morale (and,
therefore, vigilance).

CHAPTER SIX

THE CHANGING WORLD OF HEALTH CARE

The health and wellness industry has benefited enormously in recent decades from bold innovations and new ways of thinking. It has done this by not shying away from innovation and by believing in the positive power of seeking new ways of doing things. It only makes sense that information technology would intersect with the health and wellness industry in life-changing, expansive ways.

Right now, innovations are occurring in nearly every realm of health care. Check out the following list of some of these recent innovations (many of which will be ordinary by the time of this book's release).

Anti-Aging Drugs I was very excited when I read about this. Because of lengthening life spans, drugs are being aimed at aging, rather than at the conditions associated with it.

Health-Check Chair Saving time and preventing human error, this chair uses sensors to take all of a

Pepper the robot greets visitors at the CHR Citadel hospital in Belgium. Pepper is a "hospitality robot" that can provide basic information.

patient's vital signs before being seen by a medical professional.

Robot Orderlies Just as in future-oriented TV shows and movies of yesteryear, orderly robots are here! They will bring you things, summon medical staff, and even clean patient rooms.

3D Printed Prosthetics Taking 3D printing to an entirely new realm, these printed prosthetics actually fit the wearer and function durably.

Mobile Stroke Unit (MSU) An ambulance that is customized, through telemedicine and trained staff, to perform essential tests (CT scans, blood tests)

CPT MEDICAL CODING

Current Procedural Terminology (CPT), critical for communication between providers, is a vital component of today's medical coding. As medical understanding about various conditions has evolved, it has become more important to standardize the language and terms used to describe those conditions more specifically. In this way, medical coding mirrors computer coding in terms of having transferrable information that means the same thing to all parties—insurance companies, caregivers, providers, and patients.

before the patient even gets to the hospital—saving precious minutes.

In short, we live in exciting times. A promising aspect of it is how much opportunity there is to contribute.

CHALLENGES THAT AWAIT

Moving toward an interconnected future, the health and wellness industry stands to grow in ways that we cannot possibly predict from this point. What we can predict, however, is that growth of this magnitude will bring with it challenges for which we must be

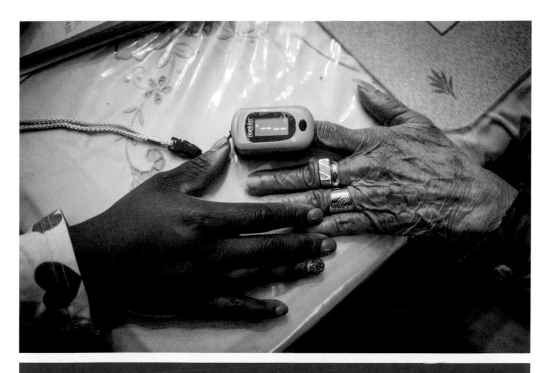

In the last few years, more and more investors have invested in health care related tech businesses. This pulse oximeter communicates directly with a smartphone.

prepared. One issue to which we must consistently direct our energies is security. While it is obvious that network administrators and such need to stay up to speed on current security measures and practices, it behooves all users to be diligent and informed about vulnerabilities as they surface. It may seem tedious to be so focused on security, but failure to get and stay ahead of security issues before a network attack can spell real trouble for all involved.

Along with network security is the changing regulatory landscape in which IT professionals must function. As we become more connected, privacy needs become more necessary and more specific. Maintaining regulatory compliance will require attention to developments in government and agency best practices (including, but not limited to, HIPAA) to understand what will be expected of professionals throughout the health and wellness industry.

Still another area in which there will be challenges for the health care and wellness industry is adapting to changes that emerge—not just in IT, but in health care generally. Nobody knows what will happen. Only a few people dared to envision anything like the internet a few decades ago. The future is full of possibilities, but what we do know is that we have to be open to

Organs that are made with a 3D printer can help surgeons get a closer look at a disease or flaw in an actual organ before the surgery begins.

learning new things if we are to make the best of it. That's where you come in.

As we have seen in this book, the relationship between coding and the health and wellness industry is multifaceted and still developing. While that development might seem a bit sprawling in some respects, it translates to an abundance of options for potential career paths. To name just a few of them, you could:

Create embedded operating systems for medical devices;

Design those very devices themselves;

Work with coding and HIPAA compliance to protect PHI and PII;

Help to manage diagnostic coding to suit changing terminology and E/M practices;

Work as an IT consultant to monitor and maintain network stability;

Work independently to connected cyberinfrastructure both in the network and between networks; or any number of these or other things. The choice really is yours, and the field truly is growing every day.

algorithm Steps taken to complete a task.

breadboard A nickname for a test experimental circuit board.

bug An error in the program's code.

code Writing a computer program in a computer language.

computer aided design (CAD) Software that helps in the design of everything from hardware to shoes.

CPT Current procedural terminology; this allows for patients and doctors to communicate more effectively.

CSS Cascading Style Sheets.

current Energy flowing through the path in a circuit.

emulator Software enabling one computer system (host) to behave like another computer system.

hardware The physical equipment used to create a computing device.

HTML Hypertext Markup Language.

loop Performing the same task repeatedly.

microcontroller The "brains" of the hardware that allow the hardware to analyze input.

operating system (OS) The software that controls the hardware.

PC Personal computer

PHI Protected health information

PII Personally identifiable information

RTOS Real-time operating system

scripting Use of a language to control another application, instead of repeating commands.

sensors The eyes and ears of the hardware, recording

events and data while monitoring performance and capacity.

software The programs written for a computer to perform certain functions

STEM Subjects for study and careers: science, technology, engineering, and mathematics.

storage Where you store the operating system and the data the sensors record.

variable A placeholder for information that can change.

voltage The direction in which the electrons would flow if two wires were connected.

web server Software written so that one computer can send web pages to another computer upon request.

Apple Inc.
1 Infinite Loop
Cupertino, CA 95014
(408) 996-1010
Website: http://www.apple.com/swift
This page of Apple's website stalks about the Swift
   programming language. It tells you about all the
   educational institutes that are teaching Swift and
   how to get started learning more about programming in Swift.

Autodesk
111 McInnis Parkway
San Rafael, CA 94903
(415) 507-5000
Website: http://autodesk.com
This site is the home of all Autodesk's products.
   Autodesk is the maker of computer-aided design
   software, which many engineers use to make their
   products come to life.

Department of Health and Human Services (HHS)
200 Independence Avenue SW
Washington, D.C. 20201
(877) 696-6775
Website: https://www.hhs.gov/hipaa
This part of HHS' website describes every part of
   HIPAA, from the consumer to the professional. It
   tells what a person should expect from HIPAA and
   how to be compliant with HIPAA's regulations.

Microsoft

One Microsoft Way

Redmond, WA 98052-6399

(425) 882-8080

Website: https://www.microsoft.com/en-us/
   trustcenter/Compliance/HIPAA

This page talks about how Microsoft's many products are compliant with HIPAA and some more
   information about how HIPAA and electronic data
   is interrelated.

Oracle

500 Oracle Parkway

Redwood Shores, CA 94065

(650) 506-7000

Website: https://www.oracle.com/java

This site talks about Java and software and a programming language. It also talks about how to get
   started learning about Java.

WEBSITES

Because of the changing nature of internet links, Rosen
Publishing has developed an online list of websites
related to the subject of this book. This site is updated
regularly. Please use this link to access the list:

http://www.rosenlinks.com/CYP/health

Culp, Jennifer. *Jump-Starting Careers as Medical Assistants & Certified Nursing Assistants* (Health Care Careers in 2 years). New York, NY: Rosen Publishing, 2014.

Joos, Irene, et al. *Introduction to Computers for Health care Professionals.* 6th ed. Burlington, MA: Jones & Bartlett Learning, 2013.

Kudyba, Stephan P. *Health care Informatics: Improving Efficiency Through Technology, Analytics, and Management.* Boca Raton, FL: Auerbach Publications, 2016.

Leavitt, Amie Jane. *Jump-Starting a Career in Medical Technology* (Health Care Careers in 2 Years). New York, NY: Rosen Publishing, 2014.

Malec, Brian T. *Careers in Health Information Technology.* 1st ed. New York, NY: Springer Publishing, 2014.

McCormick, Kathleen A., and Brian Gugerty. *Health care Information Technology.* New York, NY: McGraw-Hill Education Publishing, 2013.

Minnick, Chris, and Eva Holland. *Coding with JavaScript for Dummies*. 1st ed. Hoboken, NJ: For Dummies Publishing, 2015.

Murphy, Sean P., and Dennis Seymour, *Health care Information Security and Privacy.* 1st ed. New York, NY: McGraw-Hill Education, 2015.

Scott, James. *The Book on Health care IT: What You Need to Know About HIPAA, Hospital IT, and Health care Information Technology.* 2 vols., Metairie, LA: New Renaissance Publishing, 2015.

BIBLIOGRAPHY

Big, Nige. "Python Django Tutorials." *Mastering Django*, 2016 http://djangobook.com/introduction/

Everitt, Paul. "Pycharm: Docs & Demos." JetBrains, 2000 https://www.jetbrains.com/pycharm/documentation/

"Free Interactive Python Tutorial." Retrieved November 30, 2016 https://www.learnpython.org

Gartee, Richard. *Electornic Health Records: Understanding and Using Computerized Medical Records. vol. 2*. London, UK: Pearson Publishing, 2011.

Glasser, John P., and Claudia Salzberg. *The Strategic Application of Information Technology in Health Care Organizations.* 3rd ed. San Francisco, CA: Jossey-Bass, 2011.

Kudyba, Stephan P. *Health care Informatics: Improving Efficiency Through Technology, Analytics, and Management.* Boca Raton, FL: CRC, Taylor & Francis Group, 2016.

"Learn C - Free Interactive C Tutorial." Learn C - Free Interactive C Tutorial. N.p., n.d. web. 30. Nov. 30. Nov. 2016.

Leavitt, Amie Jane. *Jump-Starting a Career in Medical Technology* (Health Care Careers in 2 Years). New York, NY: Rosen Publishing, 2014.

Malec, Brian T. *Careers in Health Information Technology.* 1st ed. New York, NY: Springer Publishing, 2014.

Matsumoto, Yukihiro. *"Ruby."* Ruby a Programmer's Best Friend, 1995 https://www.ruby-lang.org/en/

McCormick, Kathleen A., and Brian Gugerty. *Health care Information Technology.* 1st ed. New York, NY: McGraw-Hill Education Publishing, 2013.

Minnick, Chris, and Eva Holland. *Coding with JavaScript for Dummies.* 1st ed. Hoboken: For Dummies Publishing, 2015.

Petzold, Charles. *Code: The Hidden Language of Computer Hardware and Software.* 1st ed. Redmond, WA: Microsoft Press, 2000.

Scott, James. *The Book on Health care IT: What You Need to Know About HIPAA, Hospital IT, and Health care Information Technology.* 2 vols. Metairie, LA: New Renaissance Corporation, 2014.

"SparkFun Inventor's Kit–V3.2." Learn at SparkFun Electronics. Retrieved November 30, 2016 https://www.sparkfun.com/products/12060

Williams, Trenor, and Anita Samarth. *Electronic Health Records for Dummies*. 1st ed. Hoboken, NJ: For Dummies publishing, 2010.

INDEX

ABOUT THE AUTHOR

Aaron Benedict teaches English language arts and American history at a private junior high school in Brooklyn, New York. Prior to his teaching career, Benedict worked in the high-tech industry including several companies in Silicon Valley. He also does IT consulting for the medical industry.

David Gallaher is an American comics writer and editor, known primarily for his work in comics, including Green Lantern, Hulk, High Moon, and The Only Living Boy. Gallaher has also authored numerous articles on wearable technology and served as a consultant for wellness and sports technology companies.

PHOTO CREDITS

Cover Topic Images Inc./Getty Images; p. 1 (background) Verticalarray/Shutterstock.com; back cover, pp. 4–5 (background) nadla/E+/Getty Images; p. 3 (background) Toria/Shutterstock.com; p. 5 Monkey Business Images/Shutterstock.com; p. 8 dotshock/Shutterstock.com; p. 10 Maksym Poriechkin/Shutterstock.com; p. 14 Andrei Rahalski/Shutterstock.com; p. 16 © iStockphoto.com/RayaHristova; p. 19 LOFTFLOW/Shutterstock.com; p. 22 Anna Hoychuk/Shutterstock.com; p. 25 © iStockphoto.com/gradyreese; pp. 30–31 Rawpixel.com/Shutterstock.com; p. 38 ArthurStock/Shutterstock.com; p. 45 Adriano Castelli/Shutterstock.com; pp. 50–51, 58, 62 © AP Images; p. 55 © iStockphoto.com/asiseeit; p. 60 Mandel Ngan/AFP/Getty Images; p. 65 John Thys/AFP/Getty Images; p. 67 Bloomberg/Getty Images; p. 68 Chris So/Toronto Star/Getty Images; interior background pages graphics pp. 7, 13, 21, 44, 57, 64 (electrocardiography) Johan Swanepoel/Shutterstock.com, (binary code) Titima Ongkantong/Shutterstock.com.

Designer: Michael Moy
Editor and Photo Researcher: Bethany Bryan